The Gull's Mess

Written by Emma Spiers

Illustrated by Sarah Lawrence

Rob and Bess pick up the mess.

Rob runs to get the bag.

The bag is in the bin.

The gull gets the bag!

Bess picks up a red can.

Huff!
Puff!

The red can is in the bin.

The gull gets the red can!

Rob and Bess pick up lots of mess.

The mess is not in the bin!

Rob and Bess tell the gull to go!

Talk about the story

Ask your child these questions:

1 What were the children doing on the beach?

2 Who put the red can in the bin?

3 Why wasn't the mess in the bin at the end of the story?

4 How do you think Bess and Rob felt about the gull?

5 What should you do with your litter when you are out?

6 What might you see on a trip to the seaside?

Can your child retell the story in their own words?